# THE PANDEMIC HEROES

## CHILDREN'S BOOK
## WRITTEN BY
## DR. TRAVIS HOLMES

# Introduction

The world has entered post-pandemic. The world must not forget the ongoing heroic effort, fight, and effective work that the healthcare professional continues to do. This book serves as a reminder not to forget but appreciate the significant value of our healthcare professionals. Their existence has prevented and stabilized world health and whipped it back into normality. Healthcare professionals must be respected, valued, and appreciated.

Despite the false allegations that healthcare professionals have received through the pandemic's lies, their efforts to improve quality of life cannot be overemphasized. The same individuals who have and are still believing in the false narrative of COVID-19 must rely on, depend on, and trust healthcare professionals in some shape or form. It is totally nonsense that one foolish and uneducated remark can cause people not to depend on healthcare professionals they have depended on for years. This book serves as a notice of eviction to that false narrative of not believing, trusting, and seeking out healthcare professionals for their invaluable care.

In conclusion, this intention is to educate and expose ignorance around the pandemic. The pandemic is a once-in-a-lifetime epidemic, and we need to be appreciative, grateful, and humble to have healthcare professionals who put their lives on the line to save the entire world. Let us look at this short but compelling story.

We are coming to the rescue people every day.

We are going to fight with
everything within us!

We are in this fight to win it. No turning back!

We are ready for the battle of these times.

Saving lives every day is our calling and purpose.

We have a cure and we will overcome this pandemic!

We got this. It is time to win this battle.
We will win it day by day.

It is time to fight this battle….
let us begin the journey to
become The Pandemic Heroes.

DR. SUPER IS MAKING A WORLD CALL TO ALL THE HEALTHCARE PROFESSIONALS TO STAY FOCUSED AND VIGILANT. HE STATED, "The Pandemic is still raging, but we have it under control. Let us continue to rescue and secure the world healthcare system as one of the best in the world. We must continue to fight for the common good of our society by overcoming this pandemic."

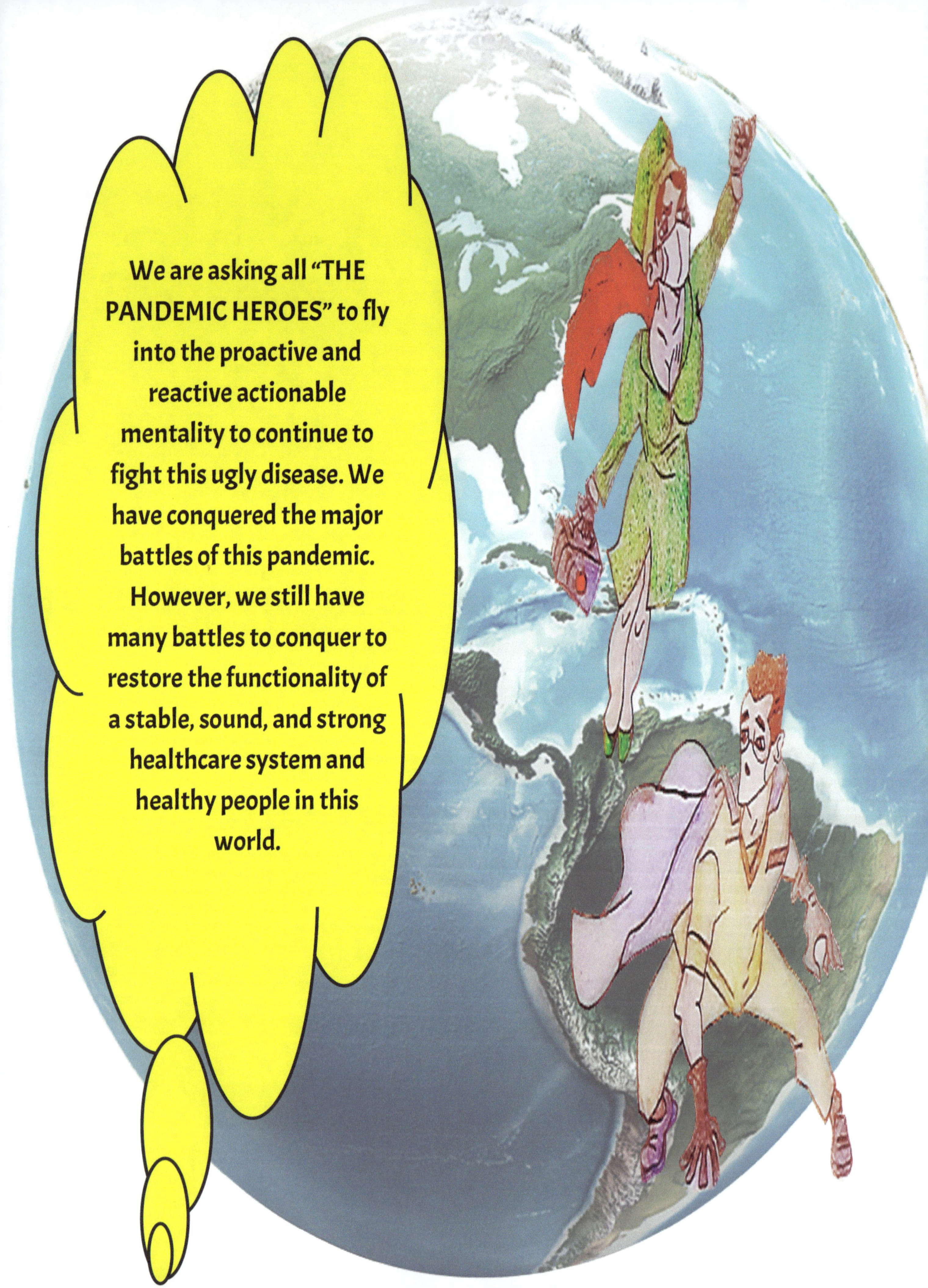

We are asking all "THE PANDEMIC HEROES" to fly into the proactive and reactive actionable mentality to continue to fight this ugly disease. We have conquered the major battles of this pandemic. However, we still have many battles to conquer to restore the functionality of a stable, sound, and strong healthcare system and healthy people in this world.

It is important to remind and stay encouraged that some people still believe, trust, and live off "THE BIG LIE."  People have been persuaded to believe, think, and feel that the pandemic (COVID-19) is a host.

No matter the narrative, we, as "THE PANDEMIC HEROES," know, understand, and have put that lie to rest every day in our fight against this awful disease.

DO NOT ALLOW OUTLINERS TO DISCOURAGE YOU AND NOT ALLOW YOU TO TRUST IN YOUR ABILITY AND TESTED MEDICAL EXPERIENCE TO CONTINUE TO FIGHT THIS DISEASE.

DR. SUPER CONTINUED TO ENCOURAGE ALL HEALTHCARE PROFESSIONALS. HE STATED, "JUST TRUST IN OUR ABILITY, TALENT, AND KNOW-HOW TO GET THINGS DONE FROM DAY TO DAY. WE ARE DISPELLING THE LIE ABOUT THE PANDEMIC."

Healthcare workers worldwide have received the call to stay proactive and reactive actionable focus on overcoming this pandemic. Dr. Super left a strong message to all of us. Dr. Super, "WE GOT THIS…JUST CON-TINUE TO FIGHT WITH PRODUCTIVE POSITIVE RESULTS FOCUSED ON FACTS AND ABILITY."

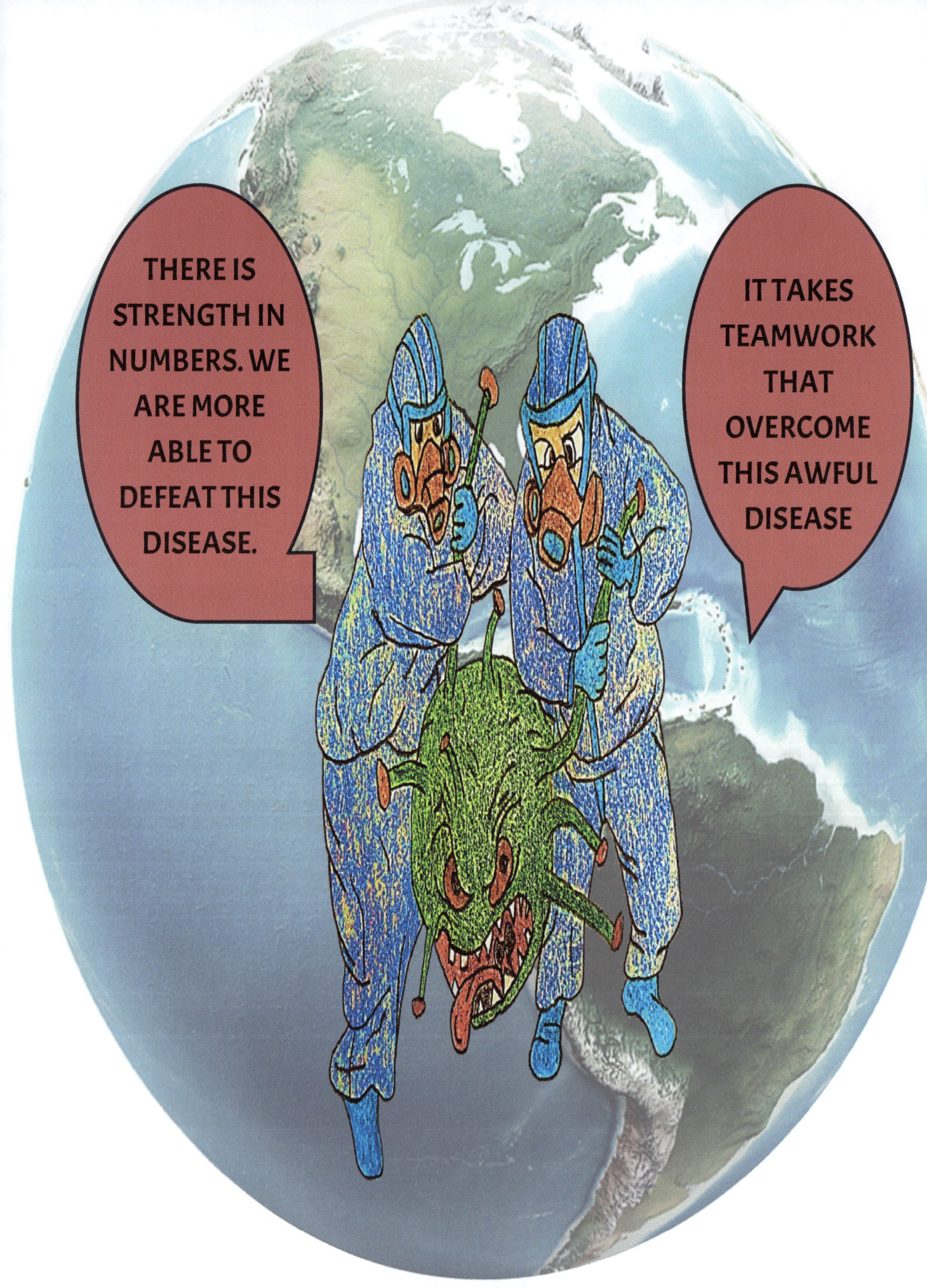

THERE IS STRENGTH IN NUMBERS. WE ARE MORE ABLE TO DEFEAT THIS DISEASE.
IT TAKES TEAMWORK THAT OVERCOME THIS AWFUL DISEASE

ALL OVER THE WORLD, MANY ARE FLYING INTO ACTION. THEY ARE STARTING TO GRIP THE WHOLE OF THIS DISEASE ACROSS THE WORLD.

THE HEALTHCARE PROFESSIONALS ARE RESPONDING TO DR. SUPER CALL TO ACTION. NURSE LOVELY WENT ON AND STATED, "WE GOT YOUR BACK DOC."

DR. SUPER, "WE ARE GETTING THIS PANDEMIC ALL WE HAVE, AND WE ARE GOING TO WIN THIS BATTLE AND TOPPLE THIS DISEASE." REPLIED, "NURSE GET RIGHT."

DR. SUPER IS MAKING A PUBLIC ANNOUNCEMENT TO THE WORLD. HE STATED, "AS WE FIGHT THIS DISEASE IN THE HOSPITALS, LABORATORIES, AND THROUGHOUT THE WORLD. WE ARE ASKING THE PUBLIC TO TAKE THE NECESSARY SIMPLE STEPS OF WASHING THEIR HANDS, WEARING A MASK, AND KEEPING THEIR HOUSES, VEHICLES, AND WORKPLACES FREE FROM GERMS BY KEEPING THEM CLEAN AND ALL SURFACES. WE ALL WILL COME OUT VICTORIOUS AT THE END OF THIS BATTLE."

THE PUBLIC STARTED TO TAKE DR. SUPER ADVICE, KEEPING THEIR HOMES, WORKPLACES, AND VEHICLES CLEAN.

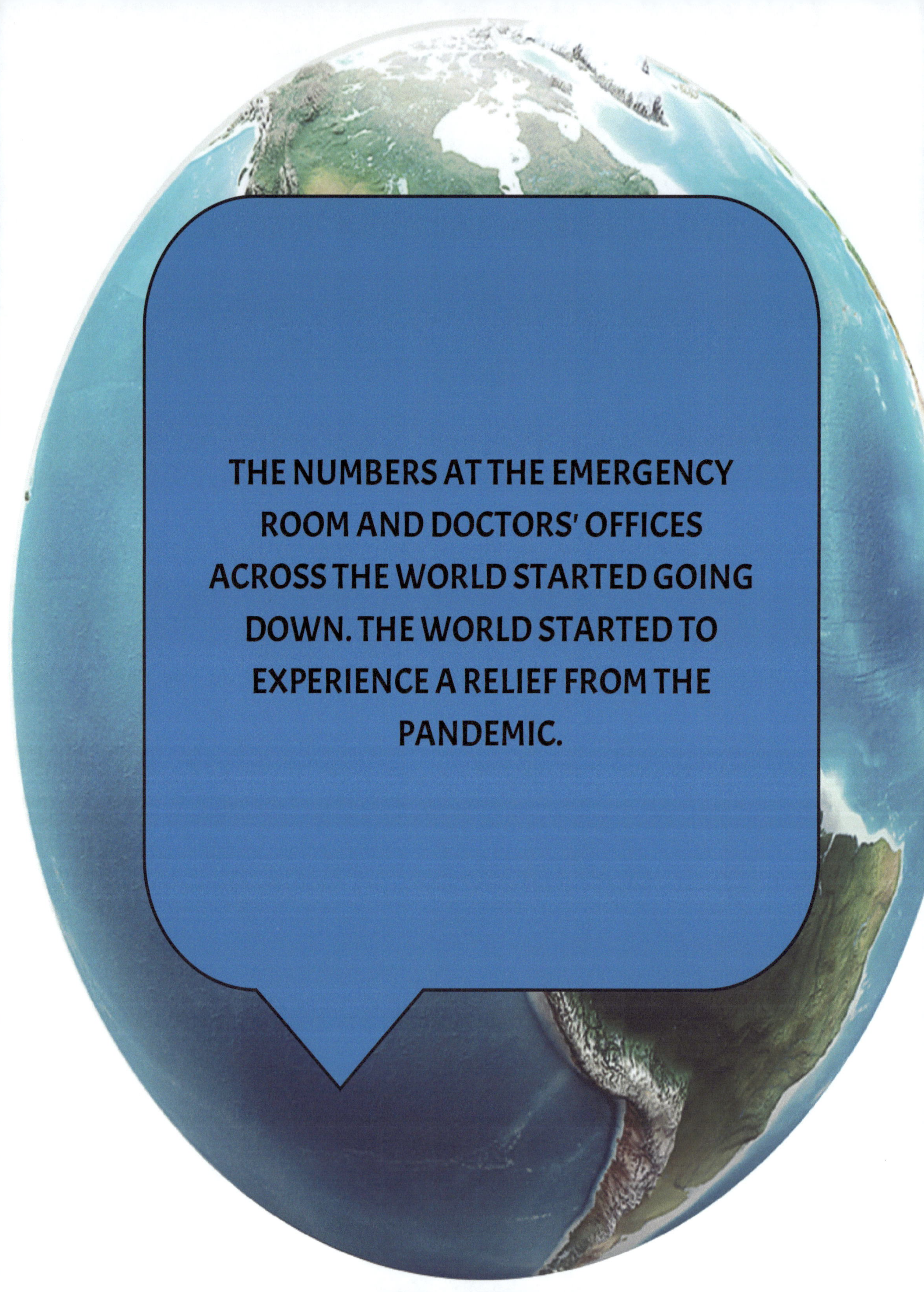
THE NUMBERS AT THE EMERGENCY ROOM AND DOCTORS' OFFICES ACROSS THE WORLD STARTED GOING DOWN. THE WORLD STARTED TO EXPERIENCE A RELIEF FROM THE PANDEMIC.

IT IS ALL ABOUT DOING THE NECESSARY AND NEEDFUL SIMPLE THINGS LIKE WEARING A MASK, WASHING OUR HANDS, AND KEEPING THE DAILY USAGE OF DEVICES AND OTHER THINGS WE USE DAILY CLEAN. THIS COMMENT WAS MADE ACROSS THE ENTIRE WORLD.

DR. SUPER STATED, "WE ARE GETTING MUCH BETTER AND MORE ADVANCE WITHOUT MEDICINE AND PROACTIVE APPROACH TO FIGHT THE DISEASE." HE CONTINUED TO ADD, "THE BIG LIE IS A MYTH. MEDICINE, SCIENCE, AND COMMON-SENSE MEASURES WILL BE WINNERS AT THE END OF THIS PANDEMIC."

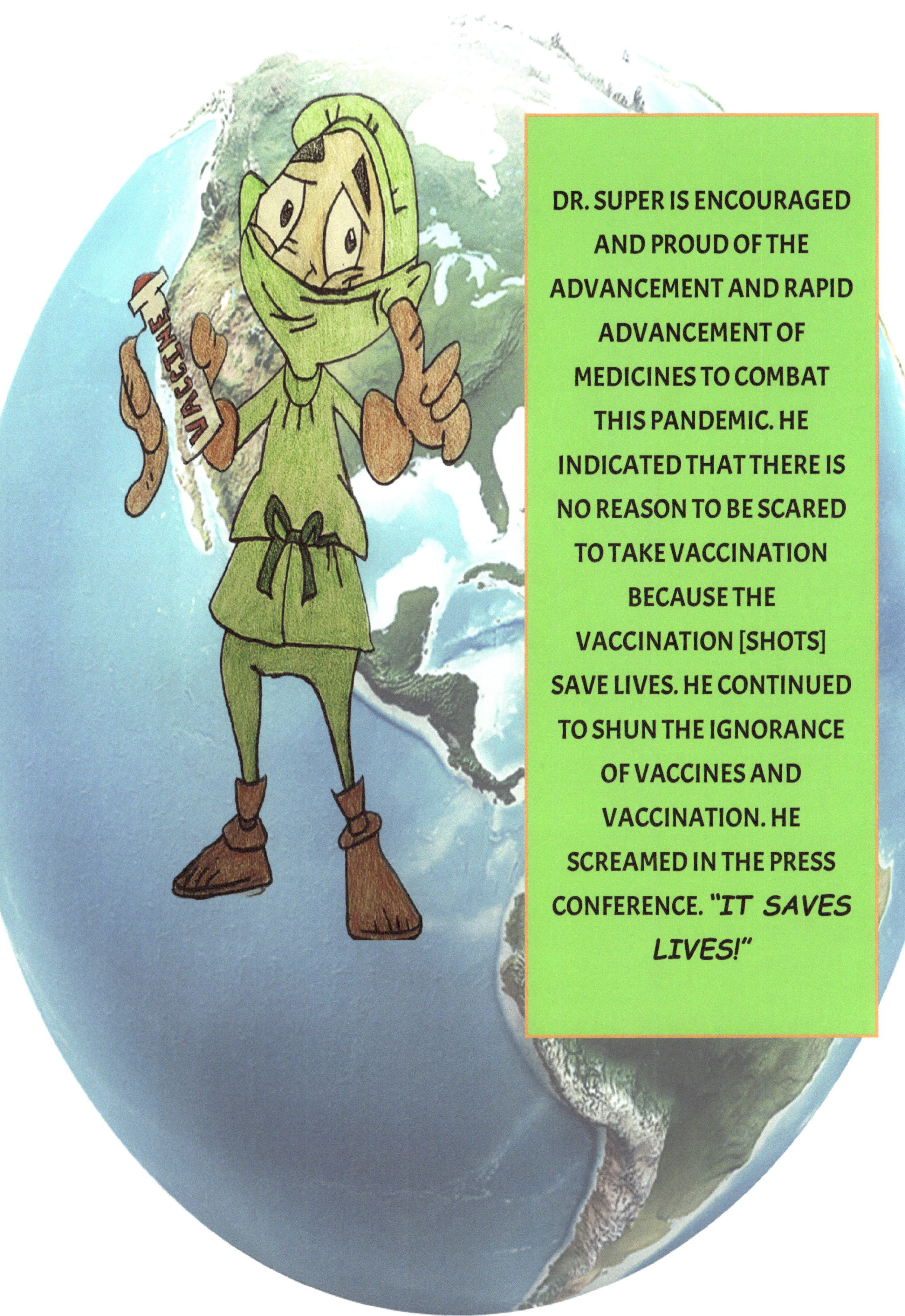

VACCINE!
DR. SUPER IS ENCOURAGED AND PROUD OF THE ADVANCEMENT AND RAPID ADVANCEMENT OF MEDICINES TO COMBAT THIS PANDEMIC. HE INDICATED THAT THERE IS NO REASON TO BE SCARED TO TAKE VACCINATION BECAUSE THE VACCINATION [SHOTS] SAVE LIVES. HE CONTINUED TO SHUN THE IGNORANCE OF VACCINES AND VACCINATION. HE SCREAMED IN THE PRESS CONFERENCE. "IT SAVES LIVES!"

THE WORLD IS WINNING THE BATTLE. DR. SUPER CONTINUED TO ENCOURAGE AND SEND A MESSAGE OF HOPE TO THE ENTIRE WORLD. DR. SUPER REPLIED, "WE ARE WINNING AND WINNING BIG."

DR. SUPER, PANDEMIC HEROES, AND THE ENTIRE WORLD ARE LEARNING HOW TO COMBAT AND DEFEAT THIS DISEASE. THE WORLD IS BECOMING VICTORIOUS AND OVERCOME OF THIS PANDEMIC NO MATTER WHAT. THE **BIG LIE IS A LIE BECAUSE SCIENCE, MEDICINE, AND COMMON-SENSE MEASURES ARE WINNING THE BATTLE.**

DR. SUPER MADE THIS AFTER PUBLIC ANNOUNCEMENT. HE REPLIED, "THE WORLD CAN TRUST, BELIEVE, AND DEPEND ON THEIR HEALTHCARE PROVIDER. YOU CAN TRUST US BECAUSE SCIENCE, MEDICINE, AND COMMON-SENSE IS OUR GUIDES. DO NOT PUT YOUR TRUST, FAITH, AND LIFE IN THE HANDS OF THOSE SPREADING AND DELIBERATELY SPREADING "THE BIG LIE." THE HEALTHCARE PROFESSION IS NOT A WITCH HUNT. IT IS SHAPED AND FORMED BY SCIENCE AND FACTS."

AT THE END OF THE DAY, THEY WILL FLY AND RESCUE US FROM ALL MANNER OF DISEASES.

OUR HEALTHCARE PROFESSIONALS ARE OUR REAL HEROES EACH AND EVERY DAY.

WE MUST HEED THE MESSAGE IN THIS BOOK. THE HEALTHCARE PROFESSION IS TRULY A WORKING EVERYDAY TESTIMONY OF MIRACLES AND THE ADVANCEMENT OF SCIENCE AND MEDICINE. DOCTORS, NURSES, AND ENTIRE HEALTHCARE PROFESSIONALS ARE OUR ONLY LINE OF DEFENCE TO COMBAT THIS PANDEMIC AND OTHER ILLNESSES IN THIS WORLD. WE CAN'T AFFORD NOT TO BELIEVE, TRUST, AND DEPEND ON A RELIABLE PROFESSION. THESE INDIVIDUALS ACROSS THE WORLD ARE OUR MODERN-DAY HEROES. HEALTH-CARE WORKERS ARE GOD'S HAND IN THE EARTH TO GIVE THE WORLD A CURE AND HEALING FROM DISEASES AND ILLNESSES.

# MORAL POINTS

- DOCTORS, NURSES, AND THE ENTIRE HEALTHCARE PROFESSION ARE A BLESSING.

- DOCTORS, NURSES, AND THE ENTIRE HEALTHCARE PROFESSION ARE GUIDED BY SCIENCE AND FACTS.

- HEALTHCARE PROFESSIONALS CAN BE TRUSTED, RELIABLE, AND DEPENDABLE.

- BEING AND STAYING HEALTHY IS A TEAM EFFORT FROM THE PATIENT AND HEALTHCARE PROFESSIONAL.